Gwen

First Published 2021
© text Casia Wiliam, 2021
© illustrations Gwen Millward, 2021

No part of this publication may be reproduced, stored in a retrieval system, or transmitted, in any form, or by any means, electrical, mechanical, photocopying, recording or otherwise without the prior permission of the publisher or a licence permitting restricted copying.

ISBN: 978-1-914303-12-8

Published by Llyfrau Broga Books, Whitchurch, Cardiff

www.broga.cymru

The Colourful Life of Gwen John

Written by Casia Wiliam
Illustrated by Gwen Millward

Gwen John's family lived in West Wales in the seaside town of Tenby. How lucky, to live right by the sea!

Gwen's father was a miserable man, and her mother was often ill. When Gwen was only eight years old her mother died, and the whole family was heartbroken.

The children passed the time by playing on the beach, where Gwen and her brother Augustus liked to draw.

They would sit for hours and sketch the shells, the fish and the seagulls. It was clear from the start that they were both very good at drawing.

When they were a little older, Gwen and Augustus decided that they wanted to become real artists so they both went to college in London to learn everything there was to know about art.

Augustus liked to show off and had lots of friends at the college. Gwen was quiet and shy and enjoyed her own company.

Although they were very different, Gwen and her brother were friends and they lived together for a while in London.

They were very poor, and sometimes they even had to forage for fruit and nuts to eat. But they were determined to stay in London and follow their dream of becoming artists.

Although both were talented, everyone seemed to think that Augustus was the better artist.

But this didn't stop Gwen, who carried on working hard to develop her skills every day. She loved art more than anything else in the world.

After finishing in college, Gwen travelled to France to learn more about painting.

At that time, it was a very rare thing for a young woman to travel alone to another country, but France was the centre of the art world and Gwen wanted to learn from the best artists.

Gwen enjoyed painting pictures of women sitting down. She used oil paints on canvas.

By this point Augustus was very famous and he was admired as a great painter. But he would say that the true artist was his sister Gwen.

For a while Gwen was in love with the world-famous sculptor, Rodin. In the end the relationship didn't last and they broke up.

Gwen stayed in France for the rest of her life, living a quiet and simple life, with only her cats for company.

This is how she chose to live, spending all her time on her art.

Gwen died in a small French village called Dieppe.

In time, people started to look at her paintings again and realised how fantastic an artist she was – better even than her famous brother Augustus!

Today her work is on display in some of the world's most famous art galleries, and many believe Gwen is the finest painter to come from Wales.

Read about more
Welsh Wonders

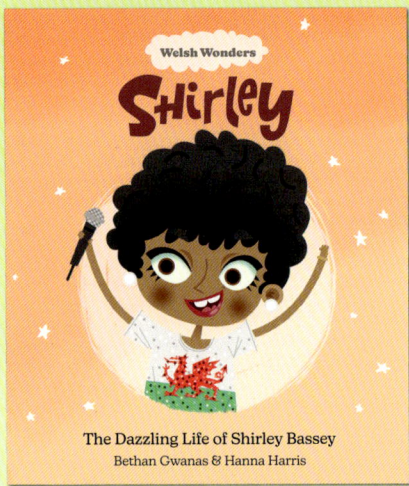

Shirley Bassey
The girl from Tiger Bay whose voice became famous around the world.

Cranogwen
Sarah Jane Rees was a sea captain, prize-winning poet, publisher, and inspiration!

Aneurin Bevan
Inspirational politician who founded the NHS and changed a nation.

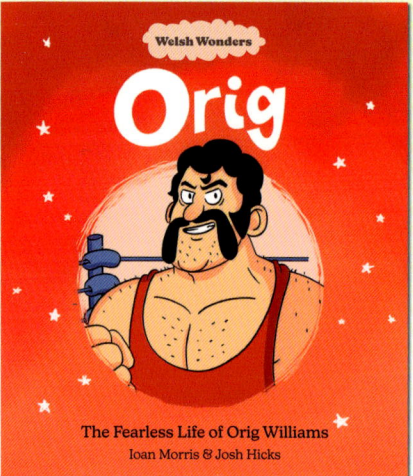

Orig Williams
The tough-guy wrestler with a heart of gold, known around the world as El Bandito!

Coming soon ...

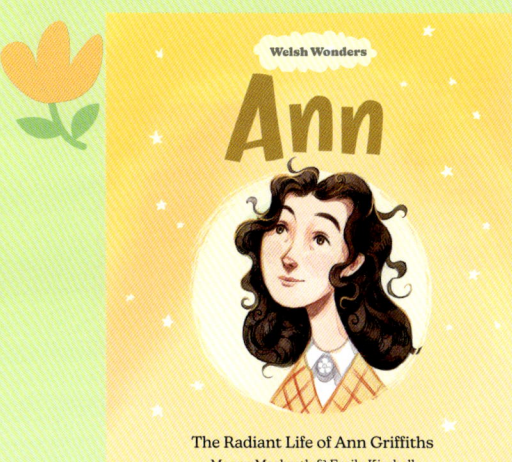

Ann Griffiths
The sensitive poet whose spiritual songs inspired millions.

Betty Campbell
The inspirational story of Wales' first Black headteacher, who fought for equality and fairness in education.

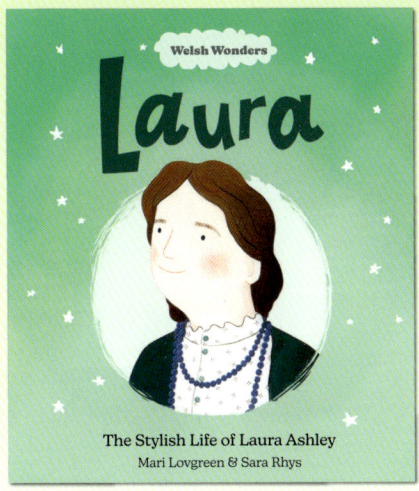

Laura Ashley
Fashion designer who built a business empire from her home in mid Wales.

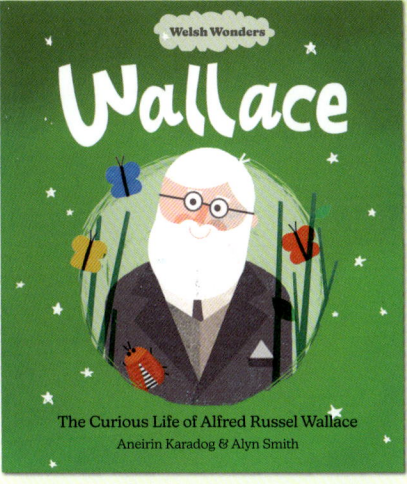

Alfred Russel Wallace
The adventurous naturalist who travelled the world and made incredible discoveries.

Find out more about other inspiring Welsh lives – from artists and scientists to people who challenged the way things were and overcame difficulties to achieve their dreams.